Awesome Inventions
You Use EVERY DAY

BRILLIANT BEAUTY INVENTIONS

NADIA HIGGINS

LERNER PUBLICATIONS COMPANY
MINNEAPOLIS

Lerner Publications Company
A division of Lerner Publishing Group, Inc.
241 First Avenue North
Minneapolis, MN 55401 U.S.A.

Website address: www.lernerbooks.com

Library of Congress Cataloging-in-Publication Data

Higgins, Nadia.
Brilliant beauty inventions / by
Nadia Higgins.
p.   cm. — (Awesome inventions you use
every day)
Includes bibliographical references and index.
ISBN 978–1–4677–1089–3 (lib. bdg. : alk. paper)
ISBN 978–1–4677–1645–1 (eBook)
1. Beauty, Personal—Juvenile literature. 2. Beauty
culture—Juvenile literature. 3. Cosmetics—Juvenile
literature.   I. Title.
RA777.H535 2014
646.7'2—dc23   2012044144

Manufactured in the United States of America
1 – PP – 7/15/13

CONTENTS

INTRODUCTION

BATHROOM BUSINESS

People will do just about anything for beauty. They'll wax the ouchiest places on their bodies. They'll keep their heads perfectly still for hours. They'll even get shots that *nobody's forcing them to get.*

And inventors of personal care products are more than happy to help people in their quests to be beautiful. After all, beauty is a gold mine. Even in times when other businesses struggled, salons have always done well. In fact, the worse times get, the more money people spend on beauty products and procedures!

Sometimes beauty inventors create a product *and* the market for it. For example, most people didn't stress about body odor before deodorant came along. Other times, inventors see a need and fill it. There's no doubt that using a hair dryer beats sitting by the stove to dry damp locks. Most often, inventors make an existing product safer, more fragrant, easier to use, faster, cheaper, or longer lasting.

Those "ordinary" objects in your bathroom are anything but. Let's rifle through your medicine cabinet and see what amazing things we'll find.

MIRROR

It sounds like a Hollywood thriller: A new technology has been invented. But only a few people know how to manufacture it. They're sent to a secluded island to manufacture the technology in secret. Any worker caught trying to leave will be killed.

Along comes a crafty foreign power. It bribes a group of workers and whisks them off the island. Soon two of the workers turn up poisoned. But it's too late. The secret of how to make glass mirrors is out!

That's right—the technology in this true story is the *mirror*. Ancient people got by looking at themselves in polished rocks or metals. Then, in the 1200s, glassmakers in Venice, Italy, figured out how to make glass mirrors backed with metal leaf. The Venetians held on to their valuable secret until 1664, when Louis XIV got his royal French hands on it.

But thank a German chemist for the mirror in your bathroom. In 1835 Justus von Liebig invented a chemical process called silvering to make glass mirrors. By the early 1900s, mirrors were affordable, everyday items. You no longer needed to be royalty to enjoy a great hair day.

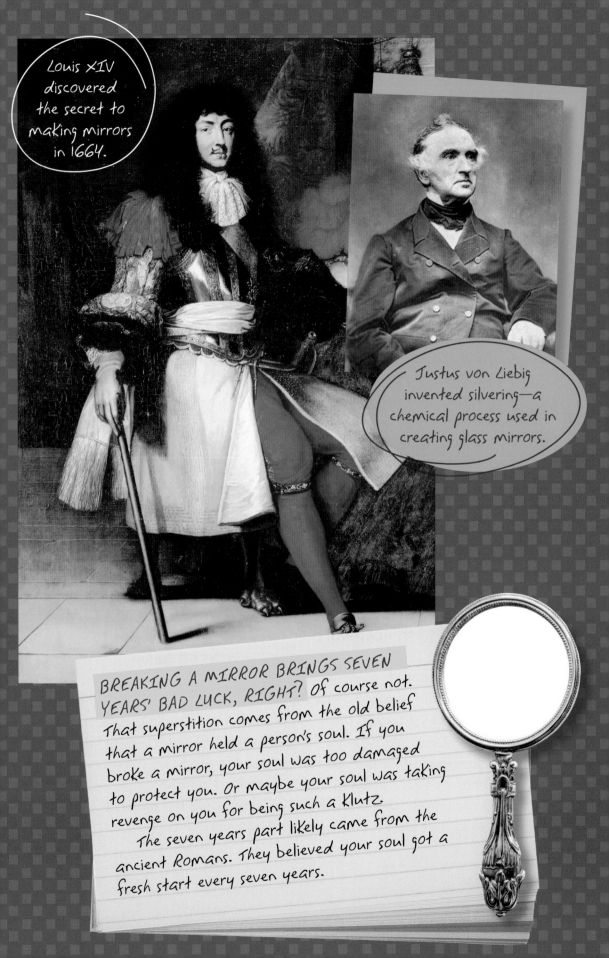

Louis XIV discovered the secret to making mirrors in 1664.

Justus von Liebig invented silvering—a chemical process used in creating glass mirrors.

BREAKING A MIRROR BRINGS SEVEN YEARS' BAD LUCK, RIGHT? Of course not. That superstition comes from the old belief that a mirror held a person's soul. If you broke a mirror, your soul was too damaged to protect you. Or maybe your soul was taking revenge on you for being such a klutz.

The seven years part likely came from the ancient Romans. They believed your soul got a fresh start every seven years.

BOTOX

Reason No. 4,224 it's awesome to be a kid: You don't have to stress about wrinkles in your forehead. And then pay $400 for shots to smooth the wrinkles out—shots that contain trace amounts of one of the most deadly poisons out there. This poison is none other than a Category A bioterrorism agent that halts the ability to breathe, swallow, and control your bathroom business!

To be fair, this stuff, called Botox, has been used to smooth skin millions of times. Most people are just fine after using it. It works by paralyzing muscles in the forehead. That relaxes wrinkles.

But even though Botox is safe, you still have to ask: just who was the inventor who said, "I know! Let's take this poison and use it to make youthful-looking foreheads?"

Actually, it wasn't that simple. People have known about botulinum toxin (the poison's scientific name) since the 1820s. German scientist Justinus Kerner was the first to name it. He called it *wurstgift*, which means "sausage poison." (He gave it that name because the bacterium that produces the poison often grows in improperly handled meat.) Then, during World War II (1939–1945), scientists came up with a plan to use the poison as a weapon. Undercover agents were going to slip capsules of the stuff in enemy food. But the plan fell through.

In the 1960s, events took a more positive turn. Eye doctor Alan B. Scott discovered the toxin worked to fix muscle spasms and crossed eyes in monkeys. Starting in the 1970s, Botox was used to relieve those problems in people.

Then, in 1992, Canadian eye doctor Jean Carruthers noticed an interesting side effect. Not only could her patients see better, but their brows were fabulously smooth!

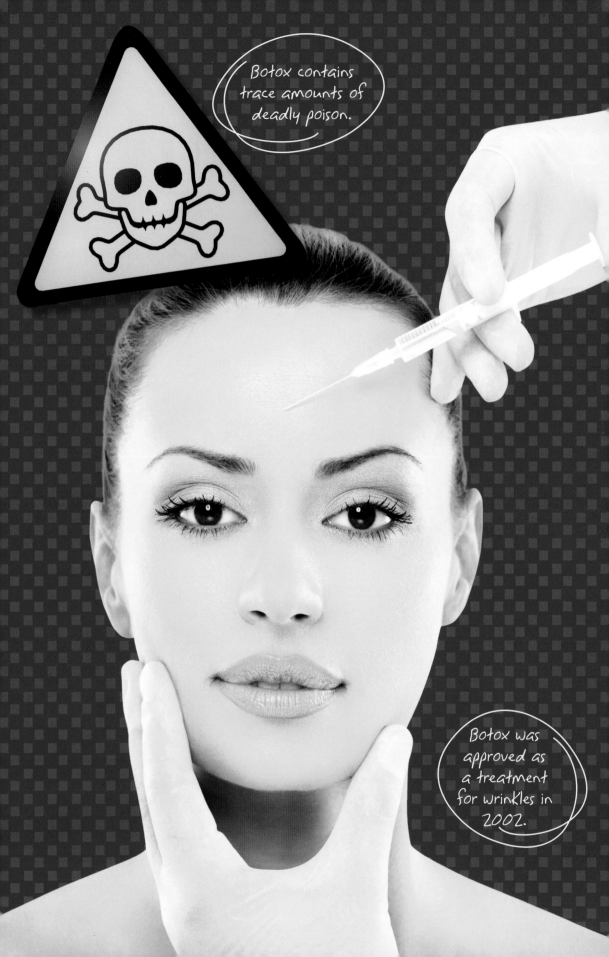

DEODORANT

Why do people need deodorant anyway? After all, until the 1950s, having BO wasn't really a big deal. In fact, for guys, it was a sign of manliness. You washed when you could. Women might wear cotton or rubber pads in their armpits. A splash of perfume handled the rest.

Deodorant did exist before the 1950s. Indeed, its origins go back thousands of years. But back when it was invented, people weren't all that interested in using it. They didn't completely understand what caused the stink anyway—namely, sweat. Or really, the bacteria that feast on sweat.

Once people figured that out (sometime around the late 1800s), better deodorants started hitting the market. One was a cream that women rubbed on with their fingers. It killed the stink but not the sweat. In other words, it wasn't an antiperspirant—a substance that stops sweat altogether. Antiperspirants first arrived in 1903.

So with better deodorant options available, why didn't people start wearing them until the '50s? Well, people just weren't worked up enough about smelling ripe. Then deodorant companies figured out a way to make them care. Their brilliant advertising campaigns started with women. Ladies were to ensure that they smelled sweet. If they didn't, they'd face gossip, unpopularity, or—worst of all—dateless Friday nights. The angle for men fell into advertisers' laps in the years following the Great Depression (1929–1942). This was a time when many people were out of work. Advertisers told men they'd better smell good to get and keep good jobs.

Meanwhile, deodorants became easier to use, gentler on the skin, and more effective. By the 1960s, no self-respecting citizen would dare leave the house with stinky pits.

An old ad (RIGHT) links deodorant to career success.

P.U.! Until the 1950s, most people didn't wear deodorant.

Q-TIPS

Sometimes the trick to inventing is realizing a good idea in a bad situation. That's how it began for Leo Gerstenzang, at least.

It was 1923, and Leo's wife was giving their baby a bath. She wanted to clean inside the baby's tiny ear. So she wrapped a piece of cotton around a toothpick and got to work.

At that point, Leo went "AAAAAHH!" and "hmmmmm" all at once. The sight of that toothpick in his baby's ear alarmed him. It also inspired him. Except for the sharpness and potential splinters, his wife was definitely on to something.

Two years later, Gerstenzang had fixed both of those problems. He'd come up with a machine that not only made safe cotton swabs. It also put them in a handy box and sealed them. The result was a completely sterilized product.

Gerstenzang named his invention Baby Gays, maybe because they would make babies much happier than cotton-wrapped toothpicks. But he soon realized his product would go way beyond baby care. He changed the name to Q-tips, as in Q for quality and *tips* for cotton tips that don't fall off.

These days, Q-tips come with a warning not to put them inside your ears. That can damage the eardrum. Or in a cruel twist of fate, it can push wax *deeper* inside the ear. Luckily, cotton swabs have about a zillion other uses. These include putting on eye shadow, cleaning between toes, and making adorable snowmen ornaments. It's no wonder more than 25 *billion* Q-tips are made every year.

BOBBY PINS

Ancient people stressed about their hair just as we do. They held their dos (and beards) in place with thorns and bones at first. As time went on, people crafted pins from wood, ivory, bronze, gold, and more. Sometimes the pins were topped with feathers and jewels. Still, for thousands of years, they were basically straight sticks.

Then, in the 1700s, wigs became a huge fad among French royalty. These wigs were so towering that women had to sit on the floors of their carriages just to keep their necks straight. Thankfully, by that time, U-shaped pins made of wire had been invented. They kept those hair hives from sliding off.

Fast-forward to the 1920s. A radical new hairstyle had become the cat's pajamas among the most stylish women. It was the chin-length bob. This hairstyle looked best with elegant waves pinned against the face.

Luckily, Sol Goldberg, the Hairpin King of Chicago, had just the thing to pull off the pinning. In 1929 he received a patent for his handy U-shaped pin with one straight leg and one zigzag one. His wonderful invention got its name—bobby pin—after the do it was designed for.

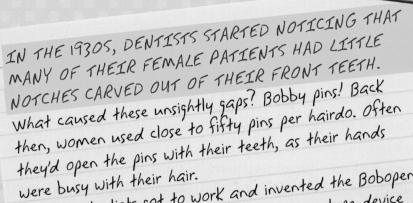

IN THE 1930S, DENTISTS STARTED NOTICING THAT MANY OF THEIR FEMALE PATIENTS HAD LITTLE NOTCHES CARVED OUT OF THEIR FRONT TEETH. What caused these unsightly gaps? Bobby pins! Back then, women used close to fifty pins per hairdo. Often they'd open the pins with their teeth, as their hands were busy with their hair.

Four dentists got to work and invented the Bobopen. Women were to wear this plastic, retainer-type device while they did their hair. It came pre-notched and everything! But the Bobopen never really took off.

This 1930s-era woman is lookin' snazzy with her hair in a bob.

LIPSTICK

Imagine if lipstick wasn't invented and you wanted to turn your lips red. What would you do? Rub strawberries on them or maybe beets? That's pretty much what people did from ancient times until the early 1900s, when chemical dyes came along. They made concoctions out of whatever red stuff they could find—including berries, roots, and minerals—and rubbed or painted it on their kissers.

But lip color wasn't for common people. It was only for the wealthy and entertainers. And during the Victorian era of the 1800s, lip color started to get a bad rap. Ladies considered it low-class.

Still, headway was made in lipstick development. First came lip color in stick form (1860s). Then lipstick in tubes came along (1915). By the time Hollywood movies made lipstick fashionable in the 1920s, the technology was almost ready. One problem remained, though. Lipstick didn't last long once it was applied.

Enter Hazel Bishop. She was a chemist and one of a handful of professional women in the 1940s. She recognized a need for lipstick that would last all day. Working women such as her didn't have time to constantly touch up.

Bishop performed more than three hundred experiments in the kitchen of her New York apartment. In 1949 she landed on her secret formula for "kissproof" lipstick. Her magic combo became the basis for lipstick sold today.

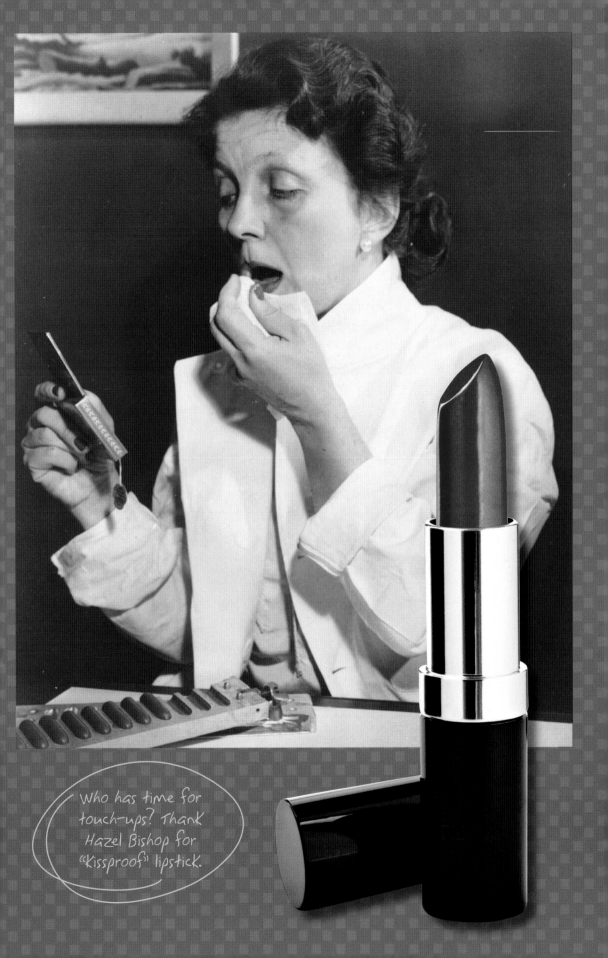

Who has time for touch-ups? Thank Hazel Bishop for "Kissproof" lipstick.

KLEENEX

"Necessity is the mother of invention." Have you heard that famous saying? It means that people invent because they have some problem to solve. That was definitely the case with Kleenex tissues.

Let's back up to 1914. There's a cotton shortage, which is especially terrible because World War I (1914–1918) is going on. And bandages are made with cotton. So a paper company in Wisconsin decides to do something about that. Kimberly-Clark develops Cellucotton. This material is made from wood, not cotton. It's five times more absorbent than cotton and costs half as much. It's softer too. Problem No. 1—solved.

Soon, though, problem No. 2 rears its (much less) ugly head. The war is over, and Kimberly-Clark has tons of Cellucotton left over. They decide that one thing they could do with all this Cellucotton is to turn it into tissues. A lot of bathrooms in the 1920s have ugly towels smeared with cold cream, a makeup remover. If people instead had disposable tissues in their bathrooms, they could use those for wiping off the cold cream. In 1924 Kleenex-brand tissues are launched for just that purpose.

But then, just as things are looking up for Kimberly-Clark, they run into problem No. 3. Kleenex isn't selling. Luckily, the company's head researcher has a sneezy case of hay fever. He soon discovers just how wonderful it is to wipe your runny nose on a Kleenex instead of on a damp cloth that you stuff back in your pocket. By 1930 Kleenex has started advertising its product as a replacement for the handkerchief. In one year, Kleenex sales doubled. Problem solved!

Kleenex evolved from a cold cream remover to a handy replacement for the handkerchief.

Don't put a Cold in your pocket!

Drawn by Williams

the KLEENEX HABIT

lets you use a tissue once and destroy, germs and all

● To check a cold from spreading through the family, put aside handkerchiefs and adopt the Kleenex Habit the instant sniffles start! For Kleenex Tissues tend to hold germs. You use each tissue once—then destroy, germs and all. Also, the Kleenex Habit saves your nose; makes irritation practically impossible. Saves money, too, as it reduces handkerchief washing.

Keep Kleenex in Every Room.
Save Steps—Time—Money
To remove face creams and cosmetics . . . To apply powder, rouge . . . To dust and polish . . . For the baby . . . *And in the car*—to wipe hands, windshield and greasy spots.

No waste! No mess! Pull a tissue—the next one pops up ready for use!

KLEENEX

A disposable tissue made of Cellucotton (not cotton)

NAIL POLISH

If Cleopatra took a time machine to our century, what part of modern makeup would surprise her most? Definitely nail polish. The ancients had eyeliner, blush, and many other kinds of makeup. They even buffed their nails to make them smooth. But until the 1920s, nobody could imagine the colorful shininess that nail polish would bring to the world.

Thank the auto industry for nail polish. In the 1920s, cars were coming off the assembly line like hotcakes. Car manufacturers needed paint that dried quickly. Gloss was high on the list too. So chemical companies developed enamels that, as it turned out, worked really well on nails.

During the next two decades, dozens of nail polish patents went through. The formulas got shinier, less stinky, easier to paint on, and longer lasting. At first, nail polish came only in shades of pink. Anything flashier was considered unladylike. Little by little, bolder colors spread from Europe. Then suntans became stylish, and people realized that tan hands look great with bright nails too. These days, you can hardly be a celebrity without your own line of funky nail polish.

THE POLISH BRAND OPI HAS SOME OF THE MOST FUN NAIL POLISH NAMES AROUND. Can you figure out which name goes with which color?

1. That's Berry Daring
2. Cha-Ching Cherry
3. Suzi and the Lifeguard
4. Are We There Yet?
5. Fly
6. Do You Lilac It?

a) sky blue
b) pastel purple
c) classic red
d) pastel pink
e) bright orange
f) dark pink

Answers: 1) f; 2) c; 3) d; 4) e; 5) a; 6) b

Can you believe car paint inspired nail polish? Who knew?

HAIR DRYER

Imagine you are a woman in the early 1900s. Chances are, your hair is practically down to your waist. You can't just throw it in a ponytail, either. That's not the style. You have to carefully wash it, brush it, pouf it, and pin it—all without a hair dryer.

It's no wonder these women were thrilled to get their hands on a vacuum cleaner. Back then, this appliance had two ends. One end sucked air in, and the other blew it out. It also came with a special attachment to hook up to the air-blasting end. Voila! You had a somewhat dusty blast of cool air to point at your head.

It beat sitting by the stove for half a day, but c'mon—there *had* to be a better way. Luckily, two companies in Racine, Wisconsin, were working hard on another invention—the electric blender. That led to a motor that was powerful and small enough to use in a handheld hair dryer. In 1920 two models—Race and Cyclone—arrived on the scene. Sure, they were heavy and noisy. And the metal casing got scorching hot. Still, it was a step up from the vacuum, right?

Early plastics started coming out in the 1930s. After that, the hair dryer took off. It got lighter and safer. Soon you could adjust the speed and temperature. By the 1960s, hair dryers allowed people everywhere to yell at one another while getting ready in the morning.

Hair dryers were a wonder when they first hit the market!

WHAT ELSE CAN YOU DO WITH A HAIR DRYER?

1. Make a Ping-Pong ball "float" in the airstream.
2. Dry steam off a mirror.
3. Remove an annoying price tag. (The heat makes it peel off.)
4. Make a baby stop crying. (Strangely, the noise calms most babies down!)
5. Glaze a cake. (Melt the frosting to make it shiny.)

These days hair dryers come with special attachments to add volume and style.

HAIR DYE

The story of hair dye is about the guy who made it . . . and the woman who made it happen. Check it out.

ACT 1: FRANCE

For thousands of years, people basically used anything they had around to dye their hair. Think boiled walnuts, flower petals, and gold powder. By the early 1900s, though, at least one French hairdresser was sick of unreliable coloring products. He went to a chemistry professor to ask for help. Eugène Schueller jumped at the chance. He turned his Paris apartment into a lab. By 1907 he'd come up with a hair dye that was safe, long-lasting, and easy to use.

ACT 2: AMERICA

It's the 1930s in America. Here, dying your hair is taboo—so much so that women make up fake names when they go to the salon. But Shirley Polykoff does it anyway. It's up to her to decide how she wants to look, right? Shirley's boyfriend doesn't think so. One night, after a disastrous dinner party at his parents', he confronts her "My mother says you paint your hair," he said. "Well . . . do you?"

Two decades later, Polykoff is the only female copywriter at her New York ad agency. She's working on a slogan for Miss Clairol, a hair dye company. She remembers that old boyfriend as she comes up with the perfect line: "Does she . . . or doesn't she? Hair color so natural only her hairdresser knows for sure!"

Clairol sales went through the roof. In 1956 only 7 percent of U.S. women were dying their hair. Six years later, that number had risen to more than 50 percent!

Shirley Polykoff's slogan for Miss Clairol (RIGHT) made it OK to color your hair.

Does she...or doesn't she?

Hair color so natural only her hairdresser knows for sure!

She wears her years lightly...happily. There's a naturalness in her looks, a fresh, shining quality in her hair that overrules the calendar year after year. But then, who needs to care about birthdays today! With Miss Clairol, it takes *only minutes* to replenish color faded by time...to cover gray with fresh, *young* tone, to keep hair lively, lovely, beautifully soft!

And that's why hairdressers all over the world recommend Miss Clairol, use it *every* time to add soft, ladylike, *lasting* color to fading hair...and to cover gray. With results so sure ...so easy to achieve, why wait another day to look younger, prettier...to feel more attractive! Try Miss Clairol yourself. Today! In wonderful new Creme Formula or Regular.

CREME FORMULA

MISS CLAIROL

MISS CLAIROL® HAIR COLOR BATH®

MORE WOMEN USE MISS CLAIROL THAN ANY OTHER HAIR COLORING

RAZOR

Look at ancient cave paintings and you're bound to learn a lot about humankind. For example, our species is really into smooth skin. But for thousands of years, shaving meant scraping random sharp objects against the skin at (hopefully) just the right angle. Ouch!

Fast-forward to 1895. King Camp Gillette doesn't just have the most kickin' name ever. He's also got a great idea. Invent something—*anything*—disposable. It's a guaranteed cash flow. But what will his invention be? He's been making lists for years.

Then, one day, Gillette picked up his clunky razor. He started to shave, but the blade was dull. He'd have to sharpen it *again*. Then it struck him. Invent a razor blade that could be replaced instead of sharpened!

How would it work? The steel blade needed to be paper thin to be cheap enough to throw away. But nobody knew how to make such a blade. The engineers Gillette went to for help scoffed at his idea—except for one.

By 1901 William Nickerson had figured out how to make just the sort of blade Gillette had in mind. He and Gillette had also designed a reusable handle. The blade clamped inside a holder, protecting skin from deep cuts. The holder bent the blade at just the right angle.

In 1903 Gillette's safety razor hit the market, and shaving took off. By 1915 hairless armpits were a must for fashionable women. Just like that, Gillette's customers doubled. His fortune went through the roof. He became the king of smooth skin everywhere.

IT'S TIME TO EXPLODE SOME SHAVING MYTHS!

MYTH: Shaving makes hair grow back thicker.
FACT: Shaving makes the hair end blunt, so stubble just seems darker and, therefore, thicker.

MYTH: Guys who start shaving young will have thicker beards.
FACT: They probably start shaving early because they have thick whiskers.

MYTH: You can shave off a tan.
FACT: Tanning happens several skin layers below the surface.

King Camp Gillette (ABOVE) became the King of a shaving empire.

Shaving with a razor sure beats shaving with random sharp objects. Yeeoow!

MASCARA

It's a simple goal: make eyelashes dark and thick. But one flip through the pages of beauty history shows you mascara's just not that easy.

The first challenge is *what* to use. You want something that will stick on well but come off easily. Starting in ancient times, people tried all kinds of stuff. This stuff included powdered lead, coal dust, walnut hulls, elderberry juice, burnt cork, melted black wax, and lampblack. (That's the black stuff that collects when you hold a plate over a flame.)

But the bigger problem has definitely been *how* to get mascara onto lashes. Sticks and needles were a popular choice. Then, in 1917, T. L. Williams introduced his groundbreaking Maybelline-brand cake mascara. This came with a little brush. You'd dip the brush in hot water, rub it on the cake, blot it on paper, and paint your lashes.

For the next four decades, people played around with the idea. There was a lotion you squeezed on a brush. A mascara "stick" to bat your eyelashes on. A metal thing that looked like an eyelash curler with little sponges.

Finally, in the 1950s, chemical breakthroughs made safe, liquid mascara possible. By then the mascara wand had also been invented, thanks in large part to something called a shoeblacking bottle. As with mascara tubes, that bottle had a narrow neck that wiped extra stuff off the brush as it came out.

All that was left was for cosmetic queen Helena Rubinstein to put everything together. Her Mascara-Matic came out in 1958. It combined the magic of liquid with the wizardry of the wand. Achieving darkly mysterious lashes was no longer a mystery.

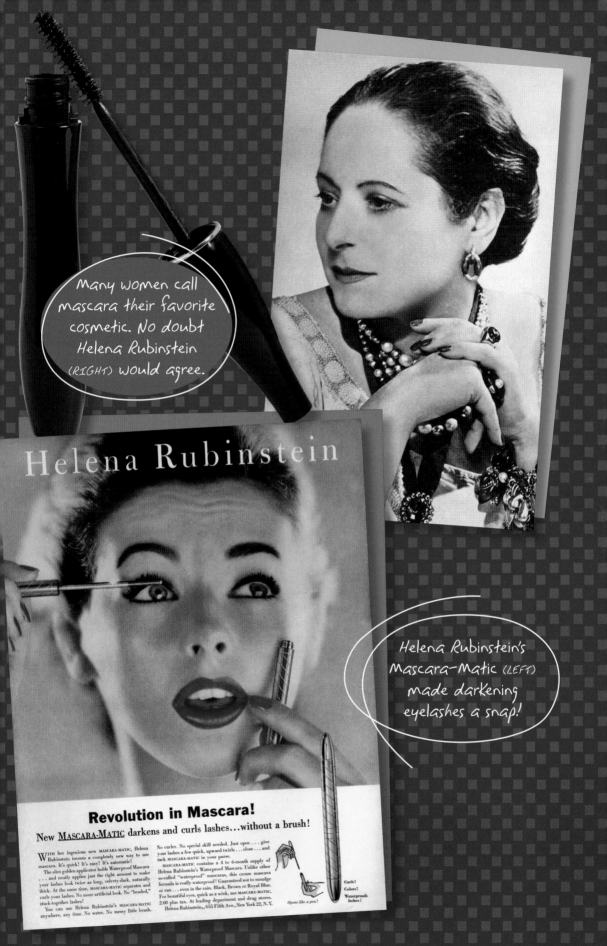

Many women call mascara their favorite cosmetic. No doubt Helena Rubinstein (RIGHT) would agree.

Helena Rubinstein's Mascara-Matic (LEFT) made darkening eyelashes a snap!

Helena Rubinstein

Revolution in Mascara!
New MASCARA-MATIC darkens and curls lashes...without a brush!

WITH her ingenious new MASCARA-MATIC, Helena Rubinstein invents a completely new way to use mascara. It's quick! It's easy! It's automatic!

The slim golden applicator holds Waterproof Mascara . . . and neatly applies just the right amount to make your lashes look twice as long, velvety-dark, naturally thick. At the same time, MASCARA-MATIC separates and curls your lashes. No more artificial look. No "beaded," stuck-together lashes!

You can use Helena Rubinstein's MASCARA-MATIC anywhere, any time. No water. No messy little brush.

No curler. No special skill needed. Just open . . . give your lashes a few quick, upward twirls . . . close . . . and tuck MASCARA-MATIC in your purse.

MASCARA-MATIC contains a 4 to 6-month supply of Helena Rubinstein's Waterproof Mascara. Unlike other so-called "waterproof" mascaras, this cream mascara formula is really waterproof! Guaranteed not to smudge or run . . . even in the rain. Black, Brown or Royal Blue. For beautiful eyes, quick as a wink, use MASCARA-MATIC. 2.00 plus tax. At leading department and drug stores. Helena Rubinstein, 655 Fifth Ave., New York 22, N.Y.

Opens like a pen!

Curls! Colors! Waterproofs lashes!

GLOSSARY

antiperspirant: a substance that stops sweating—so, it's *anti* (against) *perspiration* (sweat)

bacterium: one of the many microscopic organisms that are all around us and even inside us. The plural for *bacterium* is *bacteria*.

copywriter: the person in an advertising company who comes up with ideas for ads and writes slogans or commercials. Shirley Polykoff was one of the first female copywriters.

disposable: meant to be used and thrown away

eardrum: the thin flap of skin that vibrates, carrying sound waves into the middle ear. Keep Q-tips away from your eardrum!

enamel: paint that dries hard and shiny. Nail polish is an enamel.

gossip: stories that are usually nasty and told behind a person's back

Great Depression: a period from 1929 to 1942 when the world's economy broke down and many people were out of work

paralyze: to make unable to move. Botox shots work by paralyzing muscles in the forehead.

patent: a document given by the government that says the patent holder is the only one allowed to use or sell his or her invention for a certain number of years. Patents protect patent holders from imitators.

shortage: a lack of something, often with harmful consequences. The cotton shortage during World War I gave rise to Cellucotton, which is made from wood.

side effect: an unintended result, most often of a medicine. Side effects are usually bad.

superstition: a false belief or practice that often comes from ancient ideas. The belief that broken mirrors bring bad luck is a superstition.

taboo: banned because of social attitudes. Dying your hair was once taboo, as many considered it improper.

Victorian era: a period in British history, from 1837 to 1901, when Queen Victoria was on the throne. Makeup was largely shunned by "respectable" people during the Victorian era, both in the United Kingdom and the United States.

FURTHER INFORMATION

Aller, Susan Bivin. *Madam C. J. Walker*. Minneapolis: Lerner Publications, 2007. Walker was the first female black millionaire in the United States. She made her fortune by inventing and selling hair care products. Find out more about her struggles and successes in this inspiring book.

Colson, Mary. *Being a Makeup Artist*. Minneapolis: Lerner Publications, 2013. Get the inside scoop on what it's like to be a celebrity makeup artist. You'll also learn tips and tricks for achieving that red carpet look.

Design Squad Nation
http://pbskids.org/designsquad
Catch up on episodes from PBS Kids' *Design Squad Nation*. Check out project ideas such as "The Unpoppable Balloon." Find out how to design stuff and why it works.

Inventucation Central
http://www.nmoe.org/students/index.htm
Browse the Young Inventor Hall of Fame and learn how to enter your own invention in a number of contests.

Murphy, Jim. *Weird & Wacky Inventions*. New York: Sky Pony Press, 2011.
Read about real inventions that might have been, including a haircutting machine, a mustache guard, and a hat that tipped itself.

Rodgers, Catherine. *DIY Nail Art*. Avon, MA: Adams Media, 2013. Learn how to do nail designs such as Hot Pink Zebra and Black Lace. The photos in this guide make it easy to use. Still, you might want to pick up a bottle of nail polish remover, just in case.

SOURCE NOTES

24.   Holman Wang. *Bathroom Stuff* (Napperville, IL: Sourcebooks, 2001), 56.

24.   "Shirley Polykoff," *Advertising Age*, March 29, 1999, http://adage.com/article/special-report-the-advertising-century/shirley-polykoff/140203/ (November 16, 2012).

INDEX

PHOTO ACKNOWLEDGMENTS

The images in this book are used with the permission of: © Michael "Theaterwiz" Criswell Photography/Flickr/Getty Images, p. 5; © Imagno/Hulton Archive/Getty Images, p. 7 (Top left); © World History Archive/Alamy, p. 7 (top right); © iStockphoto.com/wdstock, pp. 7 (bottom left), 15 (middle), 21 (middle), 23 (middle); © Nicholas Musgrave/Dreamstime.com, p. 7 (bottom right); iStockphoto/Thinkstock, p. 9 (top); © Gilaxia/E+/Getty Images, p. 9 (bottom); Image courtesy of The Advertising Archives, p. 11 (top); © Flamingo Photography/Getty Images, p. 11 (bottom left); © Sergii Gnatiuk/Dreamstime.com, p. 11 (bottom right); © Todd Strand/Independent Picture Service, p. 13 (top both), 19 (bottom left); © Elisabeth Schmitt/Flickr/Getty Images, p. 13 (bottom); © Unopix/Shutterstock.com, p. 15 (top); © Underwood Photo Archives/SuperStock, p. 15 (bottom); Library of Congress (LC-USZ62-125399), p. 17 (top); © Picsfive/Dreamstime.com, p. 17 (bottom); © Buyenlarge/Archive Photos/Getty Images, p. 19 (top); Advertising Archive/Courtesy Everett Collection, pp. 19 (right), 25 (bottom), 29 (bottom); © Glasshouse Images/SuperStock, p. 21 (top); © Hulton Archive/Getty Images, p. 21 (bottom); © Superstock/CORBIS, p. 23 (top); © Yulia Nikulyasha Nikitina/Shutterstock.com, p. 23 (bottom); © Design Pics/Thinkstock, p. 25 (top); © iStockphoto.com/Nicholas Belton, p. 27 (top); © Keystone/Stringer/Hulton Archive/Getty Images, p. 27 (middle); © Michael Rowe/Digital Vision/Getty Images, p. 27 (bottom); © Cyclotimia/Dreamstime.com, p. 29 (top left); © Bettman/CORBIS, p. 29 (top right).
Front cover: © Blueee/Dreamstime.com (main); © Somakram/Dreamstime.com (brush).

Main body text set in Highlander ITC Std Book 13/16.
Typeface provided by International Typeface Corp.